99 *MORE* SCOTTISH COUNTRY DANCES

★This book is published with the full approval of The Royal Scottish Country Dance Society. It follows the successful "101 Scottish Country Dances", which is also available in this series.

99 *MORE* SCOTTISH COUNTRY DANCES

Compiled by
JEAN C. MILLIGAN
Co-founder of the R.S.C.D.S.

Illustrated by
IRENE B. STEWART

COLLINS: GLASGOW & LONDON

First published, 1963
Latest reprint, 1974

Set in Scotch Roman, 9 *on* 10 *point*,
and printed in Great Britain by
WM. COLLINS SONS & CO. LTD.

INTRODUCTION

AT THE beginning of 101 *Scottish Country Dances* the most commonly used steps, formations and methods of progression are described and illustrated. In this volume therefore, only new formations and details which may help dancers to get still more pleasure from Scottish Country Dancing will be dealt with.

In the description of the dances it will be noticed that some are given in greater detail, the number and the type of steps used being given with great care, while others are much more simply given. This is done intentionally as only occasional reminders of the steps to use should now be necessary. The basic rule is: one step to each bar of music (unless otherwise dictated) and travelling steps for movements of progression, setting steps on the spot or where movements are small and controlled. Examples of such movements are : 1. The diamond shape in *Petronella*. 2. Set and turn corners. 3. Movements where two hands are given for turning.

The Poussette is generally thought of as a method of progression but is also used as a formation where two couples move round each other to finish in their original places. This is called the *roundabout Poussette* and can be done in both reel and strathspey time. As, however, no dance in this book uses this formation in reel time, and as it is described in the publications of The Royal Scottish Country Dance Society, it will be omitted.

POUSSETTE

6

Roundabout Poussette in strathspey time appears much more frequently, and is explained below. Eight strathspey setting steps are used and the diagrams should be carefully studied as these directions are read.

1. On the first step 1st and 2nd couples dance in to take up the positions as in Fig. 1.

2. 1st man pushes outwards with his right hand and dances again with his right foot, while 2nd man pushes outwards with his left hand. This diagonal step takes them to Fig. 2. Note that 1st man and 2nd lady have had to change feet at the end of step 1.

3. Now pushing with the other hand both couples take a diagonal step into the centre of the dance. (Fig. 3).

4. Dropping the elbows and taking a close grasp, both couples turn right about to position in Fig. 4.
   This is halfway and the couples are in the diagonal line shown in Fig. 1, but have changed places.

5-6. 2nd man repeats 1st man's movements on 1 and 2 while 1st man repeats 2nd man's.

7. Both couples take a half turn to their own sides of the dance.

8. They dance one step backwards to finish in original places.

In many strathspey dances a Half Poussette is used for progression. This begins with the two couples in the diagonal line across the dance as is shown in Fig. 1 above.

1. The first step is the diagonal step outwards (Fig. 2).

2. The second the Diagonal step into the centre (Fig. 3).

3. The third the turning to own side of the dance (Fig. 7).

4. The fourth the falling back into the line of the dance but having changed places.

The Promenade. In 101 *Scottish Country Dances* the promenade is described as being done by three couples (page 28), but it can also be done by two and four. With two couples it is much the same as with three couples except that a bigger sweep is taken out to the right to begin. With four couples there is no movement to the right and the first couple should be turning to come up the middle on 5 so that the other three can get into line and all four couples can move out to their places on 8.

GENERAL REMARKS

Firstly, a word about Phrasing. Phrasing is the fitting in of the steps to the musical phrase so that each formation begins and ends with the music, and flows easily on into the next phrase. The importance of listening to and dancing with the music cannot be sufficiently stressed. The music gives the tempo, the spirit and the real meaning of the dance. Listen to the music ! In it is found the traditional spirit which the dance should express. It helps the participants to phrase the dance, to feel the impulse to dance spontaneously from one figure to another and, as the dances were originally composed to the music, it is only by really feeling the music, that one learns to dance these beautiful dances with gaiety, variety and real Scottish spirit. Too many dances become stereotyped and characterless, and because of this, become boring both to perform and to watch.

Hands. The hands are given in Scottish Country Dancing whenever possible by the natural dancer. The giving of hands adds poise and ease. It helps where a large movement takes place to a short piece of music. It makes for friendly intercourse and it adds much elegance to the appearance of the dance. Hands should be held at shoulder height with the elbows sufficiently bent to give the necessary control for a variety of movements. The giving of hands also helps to maintain the size of the set—a most important factor in a crowded ballroom.

Steps. When the Scottish Country Dance Society was founded to promote a wider interest in and to save the traditional elegance of the dances, only one step in reel time was being done—the pas de basque, and there are still many people who use this step all the time. Older people, however, said that progression could not be done correctly with pas de basque which gives a rolling movement quite unsuitable to the elegance of the dance. Skip change of step must be used where distances have to be covered and confirmation of this was found in the writings of dancing masters of the 18th and 19th centuries.

Some dancers have the habit of clasping the hands behind the back when using the pas de basque. This must be corrected, as, to perform the dances correctly, the hands must always be ready to help and guide.

The rule laid down by the Society is that when two hands are given, use pas de basque, when one hand use skip change of step.

In making these simple rules The Royal Scottish Country Dance Society has no desire to be arbitrary. The object is to ensure that all Scottish Country Dancers should do the same things in the same way, so that a dancer can go east, west, north or south and join in with dancers in any part of the world and find that what he knows and what he does, is what all the others know and do. Thus the Society urges all its members and adherents to use the same steps, do the formations as described in the R.S.C.D.S. books and try to keep the same tempo of music. Thus, and thus only, will the life of these dances be assured and many happy meetings take place all over the world.

Dress. Scottish Country Dancing is ballroom dancing and full highland evening dress is one of its charming assets. The diagrams in this book shows this attire. The ladies' dresses whether long or evening ballerina length should be white, black or pastel shades to show off the glorious colours of their sashes. These sashes should, according to Scottish Country Dance rules, be worn as in the diagrams, but on the left shoulder. As there is some difference of opinion in official circles as to which is the correct shoulder, the sash in these diagrams is sometimes on the right and sometimes on the left. The Royal Scottish Country Dance Society prefers and would ask their members to wear it on the left shoulder. Sashes should only be worn on evening dress—not with short afternoon dresses.

Diced hose for the men are also strictly for evening wear. In morning dress men should wear the tweed jacket, plain leather sporran and stockings of one colour. The length of the kilt is another important point. It should just clear the floor when kneeling. Too short a kilt is extremely ugly and looks bare and unfurnished while too long a kilt looks like a skirt and takes away from the manly appearance of this wonderful national garment. Much more might be said about this subject but these few hints may be of help.

The greater number of these 99 dances are again taken from the books of The Royal Scottish Country Dance Society and as the original or carefully chosen tunes which accompany the dances in these books do so much to enhance their gaiety and attractiveness, an effort should be made to obtain them.

Once again it must be stressed that happy, gay and social pleasure is the main object of Scottish Country Dancing—dancing must be gay or it is not dancing. At the same time Scottish Dancing has such definite forms and techniques that it must be done with poise and elegance. In fact, the more correctly one dances the more enjoyable do these dances become.

NOTE: Some of the dances in this volume are for 3 couples; in these cases a new top couple begins on every third repetition. In longer sets where there are 4 couples this does not apply. They do the dance twice and then go to the bottom. See pages 14, 17, 19, 20, 23, 24, 26, 28, 29, 30, 32, 34, 36, 37, 38, 40, 42, 43, 44, 47, 48, 49, 52, 53, 54, 55, 56, 61, 63, 65, 66, 68, 69, 70, 73, 75, 76, 77, 79, 80, 81, 83, 84, 85, 86, 87, 89, 90, 92, 93, 94, 95, 96, 97, 98, 99, 102, 108, 109, 113, 114, 115, 116, 120, 122, 123, 124.

ADMIRAL NELSON

TUNE *Own tune or any good hornpipe*   TIME 4/4

This is a longways reel-time dance for 4 couples. A new top couple begins on every repetition.

BARS

1-8   1st and 2nd couples make a circle and dance 8 slip steps to the left and 8 back again.

9-16   1st lady followed by her partner casts off and dances round 2nd couple to finish in own places.

17-24 They repeat this the man casting off and the lady following.

25-32 1st and 2nd couples dance right and left across and back again. 3rd and 4th couples do the same.

33-40 1st, 2nd and 3rd couples make a circle and dance 8 slips to the left and 8 back again.

41-48 1st and 2nd couples allemande.

49-56 2nd, 1st, 3rd and 4th couples dance the Grand Chain.

57-64 1st couple lead to the top then divide and cast off on their own side of the dance to the bottom of the set. All the other couples move up on the last 2 bars.

A new top couple begins.

12

BERWICK JOHNNIE

TUNE *Any good jig*   TIME 6/8

This is a longways jig-time dance for 2 couples. A new top couple begins on every 2nd repetition.

BARS

1-4   1st and 2nd couples set—2 pas de basque—then, giving right hands across to make a wheel, dance half-way round—2 skip change of step.

5-8   They set again and giving left hands across they dance back to places.

9-16   1st man leads his partner down the middle and up again, finishing ready for allemande. 2nd couple come in behind them on the last bar.

17-24   1st and 2nd couples dance allemande. 1st couple finish facing 1st corners.

25-32   1st couple turn 1st corners with the right hand, then partner with the left, 2nd corner with the right and giving partner left hand in passing cross over to own sides of the dance one place down—8 skip change of step.

1st couple repeat the dance with the next couple.

13

THE BLITHEST LASS THAT EVER
WAS SEEN

TUNE *Any good strathspey*   TIME 4/4

*This is a longways strathspey dance for 3 couples. A
new top couple begins on every 3rd repetition.*

BARS

1-4   1st couple turn each other with both hands
then cast off one place on their own sides of
the dance.

5-8   They turn each other with both hands and
the lady casts up and the man casts down a
place to finish the lady between the 2nd
couple who turn to face down—the man
between the 3rd couple who face up.

9-12   Joining hands in threes, they all set twice.
1st couple turn right about on the 3rd and
4th steps and finish the lady between 2nd
and 3rd men—the man between 2nd and 3rd
women.

13-16   Joining hands in threes again they all set
twice. 1st couple turn left on the 4th step
to face 1st corners.

17-24   1st couple set to and turn 1st corners then
set to and turn 2nd corners. They finish
facing the men's side of the dance with right
hands joined—lady standing on the right
of her partner.

25-28   1st man leads his partner through between
2nd and 3rd men—the lady going down and
round 3rd man while 1st man goes round
2nd man. They meet in the middle facing
the ladies' side.

29-32   They dance between the 2 ladies—1st lady going up round 2nd lady into 2nd place while 1st man goes round 3rd lady and crosses to his own side into 2nd place.

1st couple repeat the dance with the next 2 couples.

BONNIE GEORDIE'S WIG

TUNE *Any good reel*   TIME 4/4

This is a longways reel-time dance for 2 couples. A new top couple begins on every 2nd repetition.

BARS

1-4   1st and 2nd couples set twice—4 pas de basque.

5-8   They give right hand across in a wheel and dance right round to places again—4 skip change step.

9-16   They repeat bars 1 to 8 but give left hand across in the wheel.

17-20   1st man leads partner between 2nd couple, puts her across in front of him and they cast up round 2nd couple to the top, 1st lady round 2nd man and 1st man round 2nd lady.

21-24   1st couple giving right hand in passing cross over, cast off into 2nd place on their own side—2nd couple move up.

25-32   1st and 2nd couples dance right and left across and back.

1st couple repeat the dance with next couple.

BONNIE KITTY

TUNE *Any good reel*   TIME 4/4

This is a longways reel-time dance for 3 couples. A new top couple begins on every 3rd repetition.

BARS

1-8   1st and 2nd couples set twice to partners then giving right hand, cross over for 2 steps and on the last 2 bars all clap 3 times.

9-16   Repeat back to places.

17-24   1st couple cross over, dance behind 3rd couple, lead up to the top, cross over and cast off into 2nd place—6 skip change of step. All clap 3 times.

25-28   1st and 3rd couples make a circle and dance 8 slip steps to the left right round.

29-32   1st couple turn each other with the right hand and cast up to original places.

33-36   1st and 2nd couples dance half right and left.

37-38   1st and 2nd couples giving right hand in passing, cross over to own side of the dance for two steps. 1st couple are now in 2nd place.

39-40   All clap 3 times.

1st couple repeat the dance with next 2 couples.

BRECHIN FANCY

TUNE *Any good reel*   TIME 4/4

This is a longways reel-time dance for 2 couples. A new top couple begins on every 2nd repetition.

BARS

1-8   1st man leads his partner down the middle and up again.

9-12   1st lady turns 2nd man with right hand while 1st man turns 2nd lady. They return to their places—lady passing in front each time.

13-16   1st lady turns 2nd man with left hand while 1st man turns 2nd lady. They finish ready for reel of four across the dance. 1st couple back to back in the middle.

17-24   Reel of four across the dance. They finish ready for poussette.

25-32   1st and 2nd couples change places with poussette.

1st couple repeat the dance with next couple.

BRIDGE OF NAIRN

TUNE *Own tune or any good strathspey*   TIME 4/4

This is a longways strathspey dance for 3 couples. A new top couple begins on every 3rd repetition.

BARS

1-8   1st couple cast off two places on their own sides of the dance. They meet, lead up to the top, cross over and cast off one place on the opposite side and meet again in the middle to join inside hands facing 2nd lady.

9-10   They set to 2nd lady and change hands.

11-12   They set to 3rd man and move round on the 2nd step to face 3rd lady.

13-14   Set to 3rd lady and change hands.

15-16   They set to 2nd man and finish facing 1st corners.

17-24   1st couple turn 1st corner with the right hand, partner in the middle with the left, 2nd corner with the right and partner with the left. They finish between their corners.

25-28   Advance and retire.

29-32   1st couple turn each other with both hands 1½ times to finish on their own sides.

1st couple repeat the dance with next 2 couples.

CADGERS IN THE CANONGATE

TUNE *Own tune or any good reel*   TIME 4/4

This is a longways dance for 3 couples. A new top couple begins on every 3rd repetition.

BARS

1-8   1st lady dances the reel of three with the 2nd and 3rd men, while the 1st man dances with the 2nd and 3rd ladies. They begin the reel by giving right shoulder to 2nd couple and finish back in their own places.

9-16   They now dance the reel of three on their own sides of the dance, beginning the reel by giving right shoulder to 2nd couple.

17-20   1st couple, joining nearer hands, set to 2nd lady, then move round with 2 more pas de basque to face 2nd man.

21-24   1st couple set to 2nd man, then return to own places with 2 pas de basque.

25-32   1st and 2nd couples set and, giving right hands across, dance half round to change sides. They repeat going back to their places and giving left hands across.

33-36   1st couple, giving right hands in passing, cross over and cast off one place on the opposite sides of the dance.

37-40   1st couple, giving left hands, turn each other 1½ times and finish in the 2nd place on their own sides of the dance.

41-48   1st and 2nd couple dance right and left across and back again.

1st couple repeat the dance with the next 2 couples.

CA' THE EWES

TUNE *Own tune or any good strathspey*   TIME 4/4

This is a longways strathspey dance for 2 couples. A new top couple begins on every 2nd repetition.

BARS

1-8   1st couple cast off and dance down behind their own lines for 4 steps. They turn outward and dance up behind their lines to the top again.

9-16   1st couple, giving right hand, turn each other and cast off one place on their own sides of the dance, then dance half figure of eight round 2nd couple, dancing up on the last step to their own sides at the top ready for allemande.

17-24   1st and 2nd couples change places with allemande.

25-32   1st and 2nd couples dance right and left across and back again.

1st couple repeat the dance with the next couple.

CAPTAIN McBRIDE'S HORNPIPE

TUNE *Own tune or any good hornpipe*   TIME 4/4

This is a longways reel-time dance for 3 couples. A new top couple begins on every 3rd repetition.

BARS

1-4   1st lady, passing in front of her partner, sets to and turns 2nd man with right hand, while 1st man sets to and turns 2nd lady with left hand. They finish back to back in the centre facing 3rd couple.

5-8   1st lady sets to and turns 3rd man with left hand while 1st man sets to and turns 3rd lady with right hand.

9-12 1st man leads his partner to the top and they cross over into their own places.

13-16 1st couple set to each other and cast off one place on their own sides.

17-24 1st and 3rd couples make a circle and dance 8 slip steps round to the left and 8 back again.

25-32 1st and 2nd couples dance right and left across and back again.

1st couple repeat the dance with next 2 couples.

CAPTAIN MACKINTOSH

TUNE *Any good reel*   TIME 4/4

This is a longways reel-time dance for 3 couples. A new top couple begins on every 3rd repetition.

BARS

1-8   With the 1st lady leading, the 1st, 2nd and 3rd ladies cross over, dance down behind 1st, 2nd and 3rd men, cross again and dance up into original place.

9-16   With the 1st man leading, the 1st, 2nd and 3rd men cross over, dance down behind the 3 ladies and crossing back they all finish in original places.

17-24   1st couple face down and 2nd couple face up. They set and change places, 1st lady with 2nd lady, 1st man with 2nd man (2 pas de basque and 2 skip change of step). Repeat to return to places.

25-32   1st and 2nd couples change places with allemande. 1st man places his partner on the last 2 steps between the 2nd and 3rd men and goes himself to stand between 2nd and 3rd ladies.

33-38   Reel of three on the sides. 1st couple turn to the right to begin the reel with right shoulder—6 skip change of step.

39-40   1st couple cross over to their own sides, one
          place down.

1st couple repeat the dance with next 2 couples.

CAULD KAIL (MEDLEY)

TUNE *Any good strathspey followed by a reel* TIME 4/4

This is a longways dance for 3 couples, made up of strathspey followed by reel. A new top couple begins on every 3rd repetition of the dance.

(*Strathspey Time*)

BARS

1-8 1st and 2nd couple dance 4 hands across and back again.

9-12 1st couple set, and cast off 1 place on their own sides of the dance. 2nd couple move up to the top.

13-16 1st and 2nd couples dance right and left across and back, taking 1 step to each hand.

(*Reel Time*)

BARS

1-8 1st lady dances the figure of eight round 2nd and 3rd men—who stand still—while 1st man does the same round 3rd and 2nd ladies. They begin the figure by going through the middle and finish facing 1st corners.

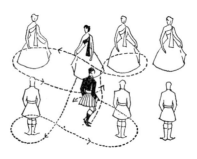

9-14   1st couple set to 1st corners. Turning by the right on the 2nd pas de basque, they face partner across the dance. They set to each other and turning to the right again on the 2nd step, they face 2nd corners. They set to 2nd corners and turn to the right to face partners up and down the dance.

15-16 1st couple, with a clap, turn, with 2 travelling pas de basque, to their own sides of the dance 1 place down.

1st couple repeat the dance with the next 2 couples.

THE CARL CAM' OWER THE CROFT

TUNE *Any good reel*   TIME 4/4

This is a longways reel-time dance for 3 couples. A new top couple begins on every 3rd repetition.

BARS

1-8   1st, 2nd and 3rd couples make a circle and dance 8 slip steps to left, and 8 back again.

9-16 1st, 2nd and 3rd couples dance the promenade right round.

1st and 2nd couples finish ready for poussette.

17-24 They poussette to change places and 1st couple finish back to back, ready for double triangles.

25-32 Double triangles. (*See page 27, 101 Scottish Country Dances*).

1st couple repeat the dance with the next 2 couples.

THE COLLEGE HORNPIPE

TUNE *Own tune or any good hornpipe*   TIME 4/4

This is a longways reel-time dance for 3 couples. A new top couple begins on every 3rd repetition.

BARS

1-8   1st, 2nd and 3rd couples make a circle and dance 8 slip steps to left and 8 back again.

9-16   1st, 2nd and 3rd couples dance promenade.

17-24   1st couple, giving right hands in passing, cross over and cast off one place on the **wrong** side of the dance for 3 steps. Then they cross over giving left hands and cast off another place on their own sides for 3 steps. On the last 2 steps 1st man leads his partner up to face 1st corners.

25-28   1st couple set to 1st corners, turning on the 2nd pas de basque to face partners across the dance. They set and turn again on the 2nd step to face 2nd corners.

29-32   They set to 2nd corners, turning on the 2nd step to face partners up and down the dance. They clap and turn to their own sides of the dance into 2nd place with 2 pas de basque.

1st couple repeat the dance with the next 2 couples.

THE COUNTESS OF LAUDERDALE'S REEL

TUNE *Any good reel*   TIME 4/4

This is a longways jig-time dance for 3 couples. A new top couple begins on every 3rd repetition.

BARS

1-2 1st lady and 2nd man change places giving right hand when passing.

3-4 1st man and 2nd lady do the same.

5-8 1st and 2nd ladies giving right hand dance right round, while 1st and 2nd men do the same.

9-12 Repeat bars 1-4. All are now back in original places.

13-16 Repeat bars 5-8 but on the last step 2nd couple place 1st couple at their first corners. 2nd lady must turn 1st lady 1½ times to do so.

17-24 1st couple turn 1st corners with right hand, partner in the middle with left hand, 2nd corners with right hand and giving left hand in passing cross over into 2nd place on their own side of the dance.

25-28   The three ladies join hands and the three men do the same. They advance and retire.

29-32   All three couples turn partners with right hand and finish ready for promenade for three couples.

33-40   Promenade. 2nd couple leading followed by 1st and 3rd couples. 1st couple repeat the dance with next two couples.

THE COUNTESS OF SUTHERLAND'S REEL

TUNE *Own tune or any good reel*   TIME 4/4

*This is a longways reel-time dance for 3 couples. A new
top couple begins on every 3rd repetition of the dance.*

BARS

1-8   1st couple cast off two places on their own sides
of the dance. They set, then cast up to the
top and set again.

9-16   1st man leads his partner down the middle
and up again. They finish facing 1st corners.

17-24   1st couple set to and turn 1st corners, then
set to and turn 2nd corners.

25-28   1st couple turn each other with the right
hand 1½ times into 2nd place on their own
sides of the dance.

29-32   All 3 couples turn partners with the right
hand.

1st couple repeat the dance with the next 2 couples.

THE DUCHESS OF ATHOLL'S SLIPPER

TUNE *Own tune or any good strathspey*   TIME 4/4

*This is a longways strathspey dance for 2 couples. A
new top couple begins on every 2nd repetition.*

BARS

1-8   1st couple dance a reel of three with the 2nd
      man, 1st lady going between 2nd and 1st
      men to begin the reel with the left shoulder.

9-16   1st couple dance a reel of three with the 2nd
       lady, 1st lady passing 2nd lady with left
       shoulder to begin the reel.

17-20   1st couple set to each other then joining both
        hands turn and finish ready to lead down the
        middle.

21-24   1st couple lead down between the 2nd
        couple, divide and cast up round 2nd couple
        to meet at the top ready for allemande.

25-32   1st and 2nd couples change places with
        allemande.

1st couple repeat the dance with next couple.

THE EXPRESS

TUNE *Own tune or any good jig*   TIME 6/8

This is a longways jig-time dance for 3 couples. A new top couple begins on every 3rd repetition.

BARS

1-8   1st couple dance the reel of three on the opposite sides of the dance. They begin the reel by crossing over and going through the middle, 1st man giving right shoulder to 3rd lady and 1st lady left shoulder to 3rd man.

9-16   1st couple dance the reel of three on their own sides of the dance, again crossing over and going through the middle to begin. They finish in their own places.

N.B.—2nd couple dance out to begin the reels of 3 while 3rd couple dance in. These two couples dance both reels in the same way without a break.

17-24   1st man leads his partner down the middle and up again and they finish ready for allemande.

25-32   1st and 2nd couples change places with allemande. 1st couple finishing back to back facing their own sides of the dance ready for double triangles.

34

33-40 Double triangles. 1st couple finish on their own side of the dance one place down.

1st couple repeat the dance with next 2 couples.

EDINBURGH JIGS

TUNE *Any good jig*   TIME 6/8

This is a longways jig-time dance for 3 couples. A new top couple begins on every 3rd repetition.

BARS

1-8   1st man sets to his partner who sets to him. He casts round 2nd man, crosses and turns 3rd lady and stands between 2nd and 3rd ladies.

9-14   1st lady sets to 2nd man, casts off round 2nd lady and turns 3rd man.

15-16   1st couple giving right hand in passing, cross over to own sides of the dance one place down.

17-24   1st, 2nd and 3rd couples make a circle and dance 8 slip steps round to the left and 8 back again.

25-32   1st and 2nd couples dance right and left across and back.

1st couple repeat the dance with the next 2 couples.

FIDGET

TUNE *Own tune or any good reel*   TIME 4/4

This is a longways reel-time dance for 3 couples. A new top couple begins on every 3rd repetition.

BARS

1-4   1st and 2nd couples turn to face each other. They set and giving right hands, 1st lady to 2nd lady, 1st man to 2nd man, they change places.

5-8   Repeat back to places.

9-16   1st, 2nd and 3rd couples, with hands crossed in front, promenade right round. 1st and 2nd couples finish ready for poussette.

17-24   1st and 2nd couples change places with poussette on the last 2 bars, 1st couple finishing back to back in the middle facing their own sides of the dance ready for

25-32   Double triangles.

1st couple repeat the dance with next 2 couples.

FROG IN THE MIDDLE

TUNE *Any good jig*   TIME 6/8

*This is a longways jig-time dance for 3 couples. A new
top couple begins on every 3rd repetition.*

BARS

1-4   1st couple cast off and dance 4 skip change
      of step down behind their own lines.

5-8   They turn outward and dance up to places.

9-12 1st couple giving right hands turn each other,
      then cast off one place on their own sides of
      the dance—4 skip change of step.

13-16 They turn each other giving left hands 1¼
      times to finish 1st lady between 2nd couple,
      who have faced down to receive her, and 1st
      man between 3rd couple who have faced up.

17-20 All 6 set twice, but 1st couple turn left about
      on the 3rd and 4th pas de basque to finish
      1st lady between 2nd and 3rd ladies, 1st man
      between 2nd and 3rd men.

21-24 All join hands in threes again and set twice.
      1st couple turning on the 3rd and 4th pas de
      basque to finish back to back in the middle
      ready for double triangles.

25-32 They dance double triangles and finish on
      their own sides of the dance, one place down.

1st couple repeat the dance with the next 2 couples.

38

THE GENTLE SHEPHERD

TUNE *Own tune or any slow 6/8 time*

This is a longways dance for 4 couples which must be danced slowly. A new top couple begins on each repetition.

BARS
1-4   1st man leads his partner down the middle and puts her across to face 3rd man while he faces 3rd lady.

5-8   1st man leads 3rd lady behind 2nd lady and up to the top while 3rd man leads 1st lady behind 4th man to the bottom.

9-12   1st man with 3rd lady and 1st lady with 3rd man advance to meet, then the men lead their own partners to original places.

13-16   1st, 2nd and 3rd men turn their partners with left hand into the middle ready for promenade.

17-24   1st, 2nd and 3rd couples promenade.

25-32   1st couple cast off two places on their own sides, meet below the 3rd couple and lead to the top. They then cast down behind their own lines to the bottom of the set— 8 skip change of step.

All other couples step up on the last 2 bars.

A new top couple begins.

GENERAL STUART'S REEL

TUNE *Own tune or any good reel*   TIME 4/4

This is a longways reel-time dance for 3 couples. A new top couple begins on every 3rd repetition.

BARS

1-4   1st man and 2nd lady set to each other. 1st man then casts off one place and 2nd man moves up.

5-8   1st lady and 2nd man set, she then casts off one place, 2nd lady moves up.

9-10   1st man turns 3rd lady with the right hand while 1st lady turns 2nd man.

11-12   1st couple dance round each other passing right shoulders to face 2nd corners.

13-16   1st man turns 2nd lady with left hand while lady turns 3rd man with left hand. They finish back to back facing 1st corners.

17-20   1st couple set to corners, turning on the 2nd pas de basque to face partner across the dance. They set to each other, turning on the 2nd pas de basque to face 2nd corners.

21-24   1st couple set to 2nd corners, turning on the 2nd pas de basque to face partner up and down the dance. They set to each other, turning on the 2nd pas de basque to face 2nd corners again.

25-30   1st couple dance the reel of three with their corners, beginning the reel by giving right shoulders to the person to whom they have just set—2nd corners—6 skip change of step.

31-32   1st couple cross over to own sides of dance, one place down.

1st couple repeat the dance with next 2 couples.

GRANT'S RANT

TUNE *Own tune or any good reel*   TIME 4/4

This is a longways reel-time dance for 3 couples. A new top couple begins on every 3rd repetition.

BARS

1-8   1st couple, with hands crossed in front, promenade round behind 2nd man across the dance and behind 3rd lady, then dance up middle into 2nd place. 2nd couple move up.

9-16   2nd couple do the same behind 1st man across the dance and behind 3rd woman and up to their own places. 1st couple move up.

17-24   1st couple cross over and cast off one on the wrong side of the dance. They lead through 3rd couple and divide and cast up into 2nd place.

25-32   1st, 2nd and 3rd couples make a circle and dance 8 slip steps round to the left and 8 back again.

33-40   1st couple set, lead up to the top, cross over and cast off one on their own sides of the dance.

41-48   1st and 2nd couples dance right and left across and back again.

1st couple repeat the dance with next 2 couples.

HAPPY RETURNS

TUNE *Any good reel*   TIME 4/4

This is a longways reel-time dance for 3 couples. A new top couple begins on every 3rd repetition.

BARS

1-8   1st couple dance the reel of three on the opposite sides of the dance. They begin the reel by crossing over and going through the middle, 1st man giving right shoulder to 3rd lady and 1st lady left shoulder to 3rd man.

9-16   1st couple dance the reel of three on their own sides, again crossing over and going through the middle to begin.

17-24   1st man leads his partner down the middle for 3 steps, up for 3 and they cast off for 2 steps on their own sides of the dance.

25-28   1st and 3rd couples, giving right hands across in a wheel, dance 4 steps right round.

29-32   1st and 2nd couples, giving left hand in the wheel, dance 4 steps right round.

1st couple repeat the dance with next 2 couples.

HOOPER'S JIG

TUNE *Own tune or any good jig*   TIME 6/8

This is a longways jig-time dance for 3 couples. A new top couple begins on every 3rd repetition.

BARS
- **1-4** All clap and 1st couple cross over, passing right shoulders and cast off one place on the wrong side of the dance.

- **5-8** 1st and 3rd couples give right hands across to make a wheel and dance right round for 4 skip change of step.

- **9-16** All clap and 1st couple cross over passing right shoulder, cast up to own places and make the wheel with the left hand and dance right round to place.

- **17-18** 1st man, giving right hand to 3rd lady, dances across to change places with her.

- **19-20** 1st lady giving right hand in passing, crosses over with 3rd man while 1st man and 3rd lady dance round ready to cross over again.

- **21-22** 1st man and 3rd lady giving right hand cross over to own place while 1st lady and 3rd man dance round ready to cross.

- **23-24** 1st lady and 3rd man giving left hand, cross over but 3rd man guides lady into 2nd place while 1st man casts off round 2nd man into 2nd place—2nd couple having moved up.

   N.B.—Left hand is given once only when 3rd man has to guide 1st lady into 2nd place.

In this diagram 3rd man shows how awkward it is to try to guide 1st lady into 2nd place if the right hand is given.

25-32   1st and 2nd couples dance right and left across and back again.

1st couple repeat the dance with next 2 couples.

THE HIGHLAND FAIR

TUNE *Any good jig*   TIME 6/8

This is a longways jig-time dance for 2 couples. A new top couple begins on every 2nd repetition.

BARS

1-4 1st couple cast off and dance 4 skip change of step down behind their own lines.

5-8 They turn outward and dance up to place with 4 steps.

9-16 1st and 2nd couples, giving right hands, turn partner and return to places then giving left hands, turn partner again.

17-20 1st man leads his partner down the middle followed by 2nd couple.

21-24 They turn and 2nd couple leading, they dance up. 2nd couple are now at top.

25-32 1st and 2nd couples dance right and left across and back again.

1st couple repeat the dance with the next couple.

I'LL GANG NAE MAIR TO YON TOON

TUNE *Own tune or any good strathspey*   TIME 4/4

This is a longways strathspey dance for 3 couples. A new top couple begins on every 3rd repetition of the dance.

BARS

1-8 1st and 2nd couples, giving right hands across to make a wheel, dance round for 4 travelling steps. They give left hands and dance back to original places.

9-16 1st man leads his partner down the middle for 3 steps, up again for 3 and then they turn each other round into original places.

17-24 1st, 2nd and 3rd couples dance Grand Chain. 1st couple face each other, 2nd couple face down and 3rd couple face up to begin the chain—8 travelling strathspey steps.

25-28 The 3 men join hands and the 3 ladies do the same. They all set and giving right hand in passing, cross over to change sides.

29-32 All do the same to return to places.

33-36 1st and 2nd couples set again and advance ready for half poussette. (*See* INTRODUCTION.)

37-40 Half poussette to change places.

1st couple repeat the dance with next 2 couples.

THE ISLE

TUNE *Any good jig*   **TIME 6/8**

This is a longways jig-time dance for 3 couples. A new top couple begins on every 3rd repetition.

BARS

1-8   1st, 2nd and 3rd couples dance a reel of three on their own side of the dance.

9-16   1st couple cast off one place, they lead through 3rd couple and cast up round them and cross to face 1st corner.

17-20   1st couple set to 1st corner, then set to 2nd corner.

21-24   1st couple turn, join right hands and turn each other 1½ times to finish on their own side one place down.

25-32   1st and 2nd couples dance right and left across and back again.

1st couple repeat the dance with next 2 couples.

JIMMY'S FANCY

TUNE *Original or any good strathspey*   TIME 4/4

*This is a longways strathspey dance for 3 couples. A
new top couple begins on every 3rd repetition.*

BARS

1-8   1st and 2nd couples giving right hands across
in a wheel dance round for 3 strathspey
steps, turn on 4 giving left hand and dance
back. 1st couple casts off into 2nd place on
the last 2 steps, while 2nd couple dance up
the middle to the top.

9-16   1st lady makes a circle with the 2nd couple
and dances round for 4 strathspey travelling
steps to the left and 4 back again. 1st man
does the same with 3rd couple.   1st couple
finish facing 1st corners.

17-24 1st couple set to and turn corners.

25-32 1st man leads his partner down between 3rd
couple, they cross over to their own sides
of the dance and cast up into 2nd place, they
dance up between 2nd couple, who have
stepped up, and cast round them into 2nd
place.

1st couple repeat the dance with next 2 couples.

JUST AS I WAS IN THE MORNING
or
THE DEUKS DANG OWER MY DADDIE

TUNE *Own tune or any good jig*   TIME 6/8

This is a longways jig-time dance for 2 couples. A new top couple begins on every 2nd repetition.

BARS

1-8   1st couple cast off one place on their own sides of the dance and giving right hand, cross over and dance up behind 2nd couple to the top. They then give left hand and cross over to their own places.

9-16   2nd couple cast up one place, cross over giving right hand in passing, dance round behind 1st couple and give left hand and cross over to own places.

17-24   1st man leads his partner behind 2nd man, leaves her on 2nd man's right hand, then crosses over to turn 2nd lady with left hand and finishes in 2nd place with 2nd lady on his right hand.

25-32   1st man leads 2nd lady through between 1st
         lady and 2nd man, they divide and dance
         round their own partners and return to the
         lady's side of the dance where they turn with
         right hand and finish facing partners.

33-36   1st couple dances half figure of eight round
         the 2nd couple.

37-40   1st couple turn each other with right hand
         and finish in 2nd place on their own side of
         the dance.

1st couple repeat the dance with the next couple.

TUNE *Own tune or any good reel*　　　　TIME 4/4

This is a longways reel-time dance for 3 couples. A new top couple begins on every 3rd repetition.

BARS

1-4　1st couple face each other, join both hands and dance 4 slip steps down the middle and 4 up again.

5-8　1st couple cast off one place on their own sides, meet below the 2nd couple and join both hands again.

9-16　1st couple repeat bars 1-8 finishing in 3rd place.

17-24　1st, 2nd and 3rd couples join hands in a circle and dance 8 slip steps round to the left and 8 back again.

25-32　1st couple dance up the middle to the top with 4 skip change of step, set to each other and cast off into 2nd place on their own sides of the dance.

1st couple repeat the dance with next 2 couples.

KELSO RACES

TUNE *Own tune or any good reel*   TIME 4/4

This is a longways reel-time dance for 3 couples. A new top couple begins on every 3rd repetition.

BARS

1-8   1st man and 2nd lady advance towards each
       other then retire, then advance and dance
       back to back—8 skip change of steps.

9-16   1st lady and 2nd man do the same.

17-24 1st couple cast off one place on their own sides
       of the dance, lead through the 3rd couple,
       divide and cast up round 3rd couple into 2nd
       place.

25-32 1st, 2nd and 3rd couples make a wide circle,
       they advance and retire. Then all 3 couples
       turn partner with right hand and return to
       own sides of the dance.

1st couple repeat the dance with next 2 couples.

KEPPOCH'S RANT

TUNE *Own tune or any good strathspey*   TIME 4/4

This is a longways strathspey dance for 3 couples. A new top couple begins on every 3rd repetition.

BARS

1-4　　1st and 2nd couples make a circle and dance 3 strathspey steps to the left. On the 4th step 1st couple cast off while 2nd couple dance up the middle to the top.

5-8　　1st and 3rd couples make a circle and do the same but the circle moves to the right.

9-10　　1st and 3rd couples set to partners.

11-14　　1st and 3rd couples dance half right and left.

15-16　　They cross over to their own sides of the dance giving right hand in passing.

17-24　　1st, 2nd and 3rd couples make a circle and dance 4 travelling steps to the left and 4 back to places.

25-32　　1st, 2nd and 3rd couples turn partner with the right hand and return to places, then turn with the left hand and return to places.

1st couple repeat the dance with next 2 couples.

KISS UNDER THE STAIRS

TUNE *Any good jig*   TIME 6/8

This is a longways jig-time dance for 3 couples. A new couple begins on every 3rd repetition.

BARS

1-4   1st couple set—2 pas de basque—then cast off one place—2 skip change of step.

5-8   1st and 3rd couples make a circle and dance 8 slip steps to the left right round.

9-12 1st couple set and cast up to the top.

13-16 1st and 2nd couples make a circle and dance 8 slip steps right round to the right.

17-24 1st man leads his partner down the middle for 2 skip change of step, up for 2, they cast off one place for 2 and turn partner with right hand for 2.

25-28 1st man leads his partner through 3rd couple, they divide and cast up into 2nd place— 4 skip change of step.

29-32 1st, 2nd and 3rd couples turn partner with right hand for 4 skip change of step.

1st couple repeat the dance with the next 2 couples.

THE LADIES OF DINGWALL

TUNE *Own tune or any good reel*   TIME 4/4

This is a longways reel-time dance for 3 couples. A new top couple begins on every 3rd repetition.

BARS

1-8   3rd couple lead down the middle followed by 2nd and 1st couples. They turn and with 1st couple leading, dance up to finish 1st couple on the man's side at the top, 2nd couple on the woman's side in 2nd place and 3rd couple on the man's side.

9-12   With hands crossed in front 1st and 2nd couples cross over diagonally to change places—2 skip change of step.

On the last 2 bars they turn to face the centre —2 pas de basque.

13-16   1st and 3rd couples now do the same.

17-24   2nd and 3rd couples repeat bars 1-4, then 2nd and 1st couples change places.

25-28   1st and 3rd couples repeat bars 1-4. 1st couple are now back at the top again.

29-32   All 3 couples dance into the centre, 3rd couple going below 2nd couple (3rd couple

56

must take a long turn so that as they dance in, they begin turning), then joining right hands with partner, they turn and finish in original places.

33-40   1st couple cross over giving right hand in passing. They meet below 2nd couple, who step up and joining left hands 1st couple turn $1\frac{1}{2}$ times to finish standing behind 2nd couple ready for promenade.

41-48   They promenade right round.

1st couple repeat the dance with the next 2 couples.

THE LADS OF SALTCOATS

TUNE *Own tune or any good reel*   TIME 4/4

This is a longways reel-time dance for 2 couples. A new top couple begins on every 2nd repetition.

BARS

1-8   1st couple dance the reel of three diagonally across the dance with the 2nd lady. 1st lady begins the reel by going through the middle.

9-16   1st couple dance the reel of three diagonally across the dance with the 2nd lady. 1st man begins the reel by going through the middle.

17-24   1st man leads his partner down the middle for 3 steps, up for 3, and on the last 2 steps, 1st couple cast off into 2nd place on their own sides of the dance while the 2nd couple steps up.

25-32   1st and 2nd couple dance right and left across and back again.

1st couple repeat the dance with the next couple.

LADY AUCKLAND'S REEL

TUNE *Own tune or any good strathspey*   TIME 4/4

This is a longways strathspey dance for 2 couples. A new top couple begins on every 2nd repetition.

BARS

1-8   1st and 2nd ladies, joining inner hands, dance between 1st and 2nd men, they divide and dance round their own partners and meet in the middle—4 strathspey steps.

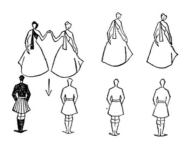

They turn each other with 2 hands to face partners, then turn partner with 2 hands and return to places—4 strathspey steps.

9-16   1st and 2nd men do the same, dancing between the 1st and 2nd ladies.

17-24   1st man leads his partner down the middle and up again.

25-32   1st and 2nd couples change places with allemande.

1st couple repeat the dance with next couple.

LADY BAIRD'S REEL

TUNE *Own tune or any good reel*　　　TIME 4/4

This is a longways reel-time dance for 3 couples. A new top couple begins on every 3rd repetition.

BARS

1-8　　1st, 2nd and 3rd couples, with hands crossed in front, promenade right round.

　　　　1st and 2nd couples finish ready for poussette.

9-16　　1st and 2nd couples change places with poussette. On the last 2 steps, 1st man places his lady between 2nd couple, who have turned to face down, while he goes between 3rd couple who have faced up.

17-20　　All set twice but on the 3rd and 4th steps 1st couple turn left about to finish 1st lady between 2nd and 3rd ladies and 1st man between 2nd and 3rd men.

21-24　　All set twice again and 1st couple turn left about on the last 2 pas de basque to finish back to back in the middle ready for Double Triangles.

25-32　　Double Triangles.

1st couple repeat the dance with the next 2 couples.

LADY CATHERINE BRUCE'S REEL

TUNE *Own tune or any good jig*   TIME 6/8

This is a longways jig-time dance for 2 couples. A new top couple begins on every 2nd repetition.

BARS

1-8   1st man leads his partner down the middle and up again. They finish ready for allemande, 2nd couple coming in behind 1st couple on the last step.

9-16   1st and 2nd couples change places with allemande.

17-24   1st couple dance the figure of eight round 2nd couple who stand still.

25-32   1st and 2nd couples make a circle and dance 8 slip steps round to the left and 8 back again.

1st couple repeat the dance with next couple.

LADY CHARLOTTE BRUCE

TUNE *Any good strathspey*   TIME 4/4

*This is a longways strathspey dance for 3 couples. A
new top couple begins on every 3rd repetition.*

BARS

1-4   1st, 2nd and 3rd couples advance and retire
twice, taking one step to advance and one
to retire. They finish ready for grand chain.
1st couple facing each other, 2nd couple
facing down and 3rd couple facing up.

5-8   1st, 2nd and 3rd couples dance half grand
chain—4 strathspey steps.

9-16   Repeat bars 1-8 to places continuing the grand
chain in the same direction, 2nd couple facing
up to begin the chain.

17-24   1st man leads his partner down the middle
for 3 steps, up for 3 and they cast off for 2
steps on their own sides of the dance.

24-32   1st, 2nd and 3rd couples make a circle and
dance 4 steps round to the left, and 4 back
to places.

1st couple repeat the dance with next 2 couples.

LADY JEAN MURRAY'S RANT

TUNE *Own tune or any good strathspey*   TIME 4/4

This is a longways strathspey dance for 2 couples. A new top couple begins on every 2nd repetition.

BARS

1-4 1st man casts off behind 2nd man while 2nd lady casts up round 1st lady. 4 strathspey travelling steps.

5-8 They turn each other with both hands $1\frac{3}{4}$ times to finish in each other's places.

9-16 1st lady casts off one place while 2nd man casts up round 2nd lady and they turn each other with 2 hands $2\frac{1}{4}$ times to finish in each other's places.

17-24 1st and 2nd couples, giving right hands to make a wheel, dance round for 4 steps, then giving left hands, dance back.

25-32 1st and 2nd couples set twice, then cross over to their own sides of the dance, giving right hand in passing.

1st couple repeat the dance with the next couple.

LADY LUCY RAMSAY

TUNE *Own tune or any good strathspey*   TIME 4/4

This is a longways strathspey dance for 3 couples. A new top couple begins on every 3rd repetition.

BARS

1-8   1st, 2nd and 3rd couples make a circle and dance 4 travelling strathspey steps to the left and 4 back again. They finish ready for Grand Chain—1st couple facing each other, 2nd couple facing down and 3rd couple facing up.

9-16   They dance Grand Chain.

17-24   1st man leads his partner down the middle and up again.

25-28   1st and 2nd couples dance half right and left.

29-32   1st and 2nd couples giving both hands to partners turn each other 1½ times to finish on their own sides of the dance, 1st couple finishing in second place.

1st couple repeat the dance with the next 2 couples.

LADY MARY MENZIES' REEL

TUNE *Own tune or any good reel*   TIME 4/4

This is a longways reel-time dance for 3 couples. A new top couple begins on every 3rd repetition.

BARS

1-8   1st and 2nd couples, giving right hands across in a wheel, dance round 3 steps. They turn on 4 giving left hand and dance back, 1st couple casting off on bars 7 and 8 into 2nd place, while 2nd couple dance up the middle to the top.

9-12   1st man leads his partner up and places her to face 2nd man, while he faces 2nd lady. All 4 set in a line.

13-16   1st man now leads his lady down between 3rd couple and again all 4 set.

17-18   1st couple turn 1st corners. 1st lady has to turn and dance up to meet 2nd man.

19-20   1st couple face each other, up and down the dance and set.

21-22   1st lady turns 3rd man with the right hand, while 1st man turns 2nd lady.

23-24   1st couple set to each other across the dance.

25-30   1st couple dance the reel of three on the sides with 2nd and 3rd couple. 1st lady begins the reel by giving left shoulder to 2nd man, while 1st man gives left shoulder to 3rd lady—6 skip change of step.

31-32   1st couple cross over to their own sides of the dance—one place down.

1st couple repeat the dance with the next 2 couples.

LADY SUSAN STEWART'S STRATHSPEY

TUNE *Any good strathspey*   TIME 4/4

This is a longways strathspey for 3 couples. A new top couple begins on every 3rd repetition.

BARS

1-8   1st couple cast off and dance down behind their own lines with 4 strathspey travelling steps. They turn outward and cast back to places.

9-16   1st man leads his partner down the middle for 3 steps, up for 3, then they cast off one place on their own sides of the dance.

17-24   1st, 2nd and 3rd couples make a circle and dance 4 travelling steps to the left and 4 back again. First couple finish facing first corners.

25-30   1st couple set to 1st corners, turn by the right, to face partner across the dance and set. Turn and set to 2nd corners and finish facing partner up and down the dance.

31-32   1st couple clap, and turn right about into 2nd place on their own sides of the dance.

1st couple repeat the dance with the next 2 couples.

LASS O'LOUDON

TUNE *Own tune or any good strathspey*   TIME 4/4

This is a longways strathspey dance for 3 couples. A new top couple begins on every 3rd repetition.

BARS

1-8   1st, 2nd and 3rd couples, giving right hand in passing, cross over to change places with partner. They repeat back to places.

9-16   1st, 2nd and 3rd couples promenade right round. 1st and 2nd couples finish ready for half poussette.

17-20 1st and 2nd couples half poussette and finish, 1st couple facing 1st corners.

21-24 They set to corners.

25-32 1st couple turn 1st corners with right hand, partner in the middle with left, 2nd corner with right and, giving left hand in passing, cross over to their own sides one place down.

1st couple repeat the dance with the next 2 couples.

69

THE LASSIES OF DUNSE

TUNE *Own tune or any good jig*   TIME 6/8

This is a longways jig-time dance for 3 couples. A new top couple begins on every 3rd repetition.

BARS

1-8   1st man casts off one place on his own side while the 2nd lady casts up one place. They meet, turn with the right hand, and return to place.

9-16   1st lady casts off one place while 2nd man casts up, they turn with the left hand and return to places.

17-20 1st man leads his partner down to 3rd place. They set. 2nd and 3rd couples move up.

21-24 1st couple dance half figure of eight round 3rd couple.

25-28 1st couple lead up into 2nd place and set to each other. 3rd couple move down.

29-32 1st couple dance half figure of eight round 2nd couple.

1st couple repeat the dance with next 2 couples.

70

THE LEARIG

TUNE *Own tune*   TIME 4/4

*This is a longways strathspey dance for 2 couples. A
new top couple begins on every 2nd repetition.*

BARS

1-16   1st couple dance the 1st figure of the
        Petronella using strathspey setting steps.
        On the 2nd step, the 2nd couple step up into
        top place, and all 4 set on bars 3 and 4. Now
        all continue the figure, 2nd couple one place
        behind 1st couple.

On the last 2 bars when 1st couple are setting
in original places 2nd couple, instead of
setting, turn into their original places.

17-24   1st man leads his partner down the middle
        and up again.

25-28   1st and 2nd couples, giving right hands
        across in a wheel, dance right round and
        finish in a diagonal line ready for half
        poussette. Partners face each other with
        both hands joined—1st lady and 2nd man
        back to back in middle. (*See* INTRODUCTION.)

29-32   1st and 2nd couple dance half poussette.

1st couple repeat the dance with the next couple.

LEITH COUNTRY DANCE

TUNE *Own tune or any good jig*   TIME 6/8

This is a longways jig-time dance for 2 couples. A new top couple begins on every 2nd repetition.

BARS

1-4 1st man and 2nd lady giving right hand in passing change places—4 skip change of step.

5-8 1st man and 2nd lady giving right hand again cross to own places—3 skip change of step. They turn on 4 and join both hands to make an arch.

9-12 1st lady dances through the arch and down the middle. 1st man, dropping 2nd lady's hands, follows his partner.

13-16 1st man leads his partner up the middle again.

17-24 1st and 2nd couples with hands crossed in front, promenade right round and finish ready for poussette.

25-32 1st and 2nd couples poussette.

1st couple repeat the dance with next couple.

LENNOXLOVE TO BLANTYRE

TUNE *Own tune or any good strathspey*   TIME 4/4

This is a longways strathspey dance for 3 couples. A new top couple begins on every 3rd repetition.

BARS
- 1-4   1st couple giving right hand in passing, cross over and cast off one on the opposite side of the dance.

- 5-8   1st and 3rd couples giving right hands across in a wheel, dance half round to change sides.

- 9-12   1st couple set to each other twice—4 strathspey setting steps.

- 13-16   1st and 3rd couples dance half right and left. 1st couple finish facing 1st corners.

- 17-24   1st couple set to and turn 1st corners, then set to and turn 2nd corners and finish between their corners.

- 25-30   1st couple dance reel of three with their corners beginning reel by giving left shoulders to 1st corners—6 travelling steps.

- 31-32   1st couple cross over to own side of the dance one place down.

1st couple repeat the dance with next 2 couples.

LOCH LEVEN CASTLE

TUNE *Own tune or any good reel*   TIME 4/4

This is a longways reel-time dance for 2 couples. A new top couple begins on every 2nd repetition.

BARS
1-8   1st man leads his partner down the middle for 4 steps. They turn round to the right on 5 and he leads her up into 2nd couple's place on the wrong side of the dance—2nd couple move up.

9-16   Ladies chain across and back again. 2nd man turns 1st lady and 1st man 2nd lady into positions for promenade.

17-24 2nd man with 1st lady followed by 1st man with 2nd lady promenade round, on the last 2 bars 2nd man casts off round 1st man to meet partner, while 1st man dances up the middle to meet his partner.

25-32 1st and 2nd couples change places with poussette.

1st couple repeat the dance with next couple.

LOCHIEL'S RANT

TUNE *Own tune or any good strathspey*   TIME 4/4

This is a longways strathspey dance for 3 couples. A new top couple begins on every 3rd repetition.

BARS

1-8   1st man and 2nd lady set to each other, then turn, giving right hand. 1st man then turns his own partner with left hand and returns to place.

9-16   1st lady does the same but she turns 2nd man with left hand then partner with right hand and returns to her place.

17-20   1st man leads his partner down between 2nd couple, they divide and dance round behind 3rd couple, meeting below 3rd couple to turn each other with 2 hands.

21-24   1st couple dance up to the top, cast off one place on their own sides of the dance, and cross over to face 1st corners.

25-28   1st couple set to corners—4 setting steps.

29-32   1st couple turn each other with both hands 1½ times to finish on their own side of the dance, one place down.

1st couple repeat the dance with next 2 couples.

LORD EGLINTON'S REEL

TUNE *Any good reel*   TIME 4/4

This is a longways reel-time dance for 3 couples. A new top couple begins on every 3rd repetition.

BARS

1-8   1st couple set to each other and cast off two places on their own sides of the dance. Repeat back to place.

9-16   1st man leads his partner down the middle for 3 steps, up for 3 and they cast off into 2nd place on their own sides of the dance with 2 steps.

17-24   1st, 2nd and 3rd couples make a circle and dance round 8 slip steps to the left and 8 back again.

25-28   1st, 2nd and 3rd ladies join hands and the 3 men do the same. All advance and retire—4 skip change of step.

29-32   All turn partners with both hands and 4 pas de basque.

1st couple repeat the dance with the next 2 couples.

McLACHLAN'S REEL

TUNE *Any good strathspey*　　　　　　　TIME 4/4

This is a longways strathspey dance for 3 couples. A new top couple begins on every 3rd repetition.

BARS

1-8　1st man leads his partner down the middle for 3 steps, up for 3 and they cast off one place on their own sides for 2 steps.

9-16　1st man leads his partner down the middle again for 3 steps, up for 3 into 2nd place and they cast off into 3rd place.

17-24　1st, 2nd and 3rd couples make a circle and dance 4 travelling steps to the left and 4 back again.

25-28　1st couple dance up to the top and cast off one place on their own sides of the dance.

29-32　1st and 2nd couples dance right and left across and back taking one step to each hand.

1st couple repeat the dance with the next 2 couples.

MAGGIE LAUDER

TUNE *Original or any good strathspey*   TIME 4/4

This is a longways strathspey dance for 2 couples. A new top couple begins on every 2nd repetition.

BARS

1-4   1st and 2nd couples set twice—4 strathspey setting steps.

5-8   1st and 2nd couples giving right hands across in a wheel, dance half way round to change sides—4 travelling steps.

9-16   1st and 2nd couples repeat bars 1-8 but give left hands in the wheel.

17-24   1st man leads his partner down the middle for 3 steps, up for 3 and they cast off one place on their own sides for 2 steps.

25-32   1st and 2nd couples dance right and left across and back again.

1st couple repeat the dance with next couple.

THE MARQUIS OF LORNE

TUNE *Any good strathspey*   TIME **4/4**

This is a longways strathspey dance for 3 couples. A new top couple begins on every 3rd repetition.

BARS

1-8   1st man leads his partner down the middle followed by 2nd couple—4 strathspey steps. They turn and 2nd couple leads up into top couple's place while 1st couple finish in 2nd place.

9-16   1st, 2nd and 3rd couples make a circle and dance 4 steps round to the left and 4 back again to places. They finish ready for Grand Chain, 2nd couple facing each other at top, 1st couple facing down and 3rd couple facing up.

17-24 Grand Chain.

25-32 1st couple set to each other twice then 1st man leads his partner through 3rd couple. They divide and dance up round 3rd couple into 2nd place on their own sides of the dance.

1st couple repeat the dance with next 2 couples.

MAXWELL'S RANT

TUNE *Own tune or any good reel*   TIME 4/4

This is a longways reel-time dance for 3 couples. A new couple begins on every 3rd repetition.

BARS

1-8   1st couple dance reel of three on the opposite sides of the dance. They begin the reel by crossing over and going through the middle, 1st man giving right shoulder to 3rd lady and 1st lady left shoulder to 3rd man.

9-16   1st couple dance reel of three on their own sides again, crossing over and going through the middle to begin.

17-20   1st couple, giving right hand in passing, cross over and cast off one place.

21-24   They dance half figure of eight round 2nd couple, who have stepped up to the top. They finish in 2nd place on their own side.

25-28   1st man leads his partner down the middle, they divide and cast up round 3rd couple into 2nd place.

29-32   2nd, 1st and 3rd couples turn each other with right hand and return to place.

1st couple repeat the dance with the next 2 couples.

THE MERRY REAPERS

TUNE *Any good jig*   TIME 6/8

This is a longways jig-time dance for 3 couples. A new top couple begins on every 3rd repetition.

BARS

1-8   1st couple cast off two places on their own sides, meet below 3rd couple, lead up the middle and cast off on their own sides into 2nd place. 2nd couple move up.

9-16   1st, 2nd and 3rd couples make a circle and dance 8 slip steps round to the left and 8 back to the right to places.

17-24   1st, 2nd and 3rd couples turn partner with right hand and return to place for 4 skip change of steps, then repeat giving left hand.

1st couple repeat the dance with the next 2 couples.

MISS BURNS' REEL

TUNE *Own tune or any good reel*   TIME 4/4

This is a longways reel-time dance for 2 couples. A new top couple begins on every 2nd repetition.

BARS
1-4   1st couple turn each other with right hand for 1½ times.

5-8   1st man turns 2nd lady with left hand while 1st lady turns 2nd man with left hand.

9-12   1st man turns 2nd lady with the right hand while 1st lady turns 2nd man also with right hand.

13-16   1st couple turn each other with left hand 1½ times to original places.

17-24   1st man leads his partner down the middle and up again.

25-32   1st and 2nd couples change places with poussette.

1st couple repeat the dance with the next couple.

MISS BETTY BOYLE'S REEL

TUNE *Any good strathspey*   TIME 4/4

*This is a longways strathspey dance for 3 couples. A
new top couple begins on every 3rd repetition.*

BARS

1-4   1st and 2nd couples set to partner, then
      joining right hand in passing, cross over to
      change places.

5-8   They repeat this back to places.

9-16 1st man leads his partner down the middle
      and up again, placing her between the 2nd
      couple who have turned to face down, and
      finishing himself between 3rd couple who
      have faced up. They join hands 3 and 3.

17-20 All set twice—4 strathspey setting steps but
       on the 3rd and 4th steps, 1st couple turn left
       about to finish lady between 2nd and 3rd
       ladies, and man between 2nd and 3rd men.
       Join hands in 3's again.

21-24 They all set twice.

25-32 1st, 2nd and 3rd couples make a circle and
       dance 4 strathspey travelling steps round to
       the left and 4 back to the right.

1st couple repeat the dance with the next 2 couples.

MISS CHOLMONDELEY'S REEL

TUNE *Any good reel tune* TIME 4/4

*This is a longways reel-time dance for 3 couples. A new
top couple begins on every 3rd repetition.*

BARS

1-8   1st couple promenade round 2nd couple and
finish in 2nd place—8 skip change of step.
2nd couple move up.

9-16   2nd couple promenade round 1st couple and
finish in own place. 1st couple move up.

17-24 1st man leads his partner down the middle for
4 skip change of step, turns on 5, leads up on
6. They divide and dance round behind the
3rd couple into 2nd place. 2nd couple move
up.

25-32 1st and 2nd couples dance right and left
across and back again.

1st couple repeats the dance with the next couple.

MISS CHIRSTY STEWART

TUNE *Own tune or any good reel*   TIME 4/4

This is a longways reel-time dance for 3 couples. A new top couple begins on every 3rd repetition.

BARS

1-4   1st and 2nd couples dance half right and left across to the opposite side.

5-6   1st couple giving right hand turn into the middle of the dance, while 2nd couple giving right hand, cross over to own side, turning round by the right to join left hands with 1st couple.

7-8   All set in line and finish facing down the dance, 1st and 2nd ladies turning by the right on bar 8.

9-16   All 4 dance down the middle and up again.

17-24   Reel of four across the dance, 1st couple finish facing 1st corners.

25-32   They turn 1st corners with the right hand, partners in the middle with the left, 2nd corners with right hand, and, giving partner left hand in passing, cross over to own sides one place down.

1st couple repeat the dance with next 2 couples.

MISS CLEMY STEWART'S REEL

TUNE *Own tune or any good reel*   TIME **4/4**

This is a longways reel-time dance for 3 couples. A new top couple begins on every 3rd repetition.

BARS

1-4   1st man casts off behind 2nd man and crosses over—2 skip change of step—then turns 3rd lady with 2 hands and 2 pas de basque. He finishes standing between 2nd and 3rd ladies.

5-8   1st lady casts off behind 2nd lady, turns 3rd man and finishes between 2nd and 3rd men.

9-12   1st and 2nd couple give right hands across to make a wheel and dance round for 4 steps.

13-16   1st and 3rd couple give left hands across and dance back, 1st couple finish facing 1st corners.

17-24   1st couple set to and turn corners. They finish between corners.

25-30   They dance reel of three with their corners, beginning the reel by giving left shoulders to 1st corners.

31-32   1st couple cross over to own sides of the dance one place down.

1st couple repeat the dance with the next 2 couples.

MISS CORBETT'S STRATHSPEY

TUNE *Own tune or any good strathspey*   TIME 4/4

This is a longways strathspey dance for 3 couples. A new top couple begins on every 3rd repetition.

BARS

1-2   1st man and 2nd lady, giving right hand in passing, change places.

3-4   1st lady and 2nd man do the same.

5-8   1st man and 3rd man, then 1st lady and 3rd lady, do the same.

9-12   All 3 couples set twice to partners.

13-16   1st couple turn each other with 2 hands, while 2nd and 3rd couples dance half right and left. All are now on their own sides of the dance. 1st and 2nd couple face up for reels of three.

17-24   Reels of three on the sides of the dance.

25-28   1st couple cast up, followed by 2nd and 3rd couples. At the top the 1st couple cast off into 2nd place while 2nd couple dance up to the top.

29-32   All 3 couples turn partners with 2 hands.

1st couple repeat the dance with the next 2 couples.

TUNE *Own tune or any good reel*   TIME 4/4

This is a longways reel-time dance for 2 couples. A new top couple begins on every 2nd repetition.

BARS

1-8 1st and 2nd couples set and giving right hand in passing, cross over to change places. They repeat back to place.

9-16 1st and 2nd couples, giving right hands across to make a wheel, dance round for 3 steps, turn and giving left hands across dance back for 3 then on the last two bars 1st couple cast off into 2nd place while 2nd couple dance up to the top.

17-24 1st couple cross over giving right hand in passing and cast up one place on the wrong side, then, giving left hand in passing, cross over to own sides and cast down into 2nd place.

25-32 1st and 2nd couples dance right and left across and back again.

1st couple repeat the dance with next couple.

MISS MARGARET HILL

TUNE *Any good jig*   TIME 6/8

This is a longways jig-time dance for 3 couples. A new top couple begins on every 3rd repetition.

BARS

1-4 1st lady advances towards 2nd man with 2 pas de basque but passes on and turns 3rd man with both hands and finishes standing between 2nd and 3rd men—2 pas de basque.

5-8 1st man does the same with 2nd and 3rd ladies but finishes hand in hand in the middle with his partner who has crossed over to her own side on the last step.

9-16 1st man leads his partner down the middle and up to the top. They finish ready for allemande.

17-24 1st and 2nd couples allemande. 1st couple finish facing 1st corners.

25-32 They turn 1st corner with the right hand, partners in the middle with the left, 2nd corners with the right and giving left hand in passing, cross over to their own side of the dance one place down.

1st couple repeat the dance with next 2 couples.

MISS WELSH'S REEL

TUNE *The Campbells are Coming or any good jig*

TIME 6/8

This is a longways jig-time dance for 3 couples. A new top couple begins on every 3rd repetition.

BARS

1-8 1st and 2nd couples set with 2 pas de basque and giving partner right hand, cross over to change places—2 skip change of step. They repeat this back to place.

9-16 1st and 2nd couples give right hands across to make a wheel and dance round for 4 skip change of step. They give left hands and dance back to original places.

17-24 1st man leads his partner down the middle for 4 steps. They turn on 5 and come up to face 1st corners. 2nd couple move up.

25-32 1st couple turn 1st corner with right hand, then partner in the middle with left. They turn 2nd corner with the right and, giving left hand to partner in passing, cross over to own sides of the dance one place down.

1st couple repeat the dance with the next 2 couples.

THE MONIFIETH STAR

TUNE *Any good reel*   TIME 4/4

This is a longways reel-time dance for 2 couples. A new top couple begins on every 2nd repetition.

BARS

1-8   1st couple make a circle with 2nd lady and dance 8 slip steps round to the left and 8 back again. They finish in a diagonal line ready for a reel of three.

9-16   1st couple dance reel of three with 2nd lady and finish facing 2nd man.

17-32 1st couple repeat bars 1-16 with 2nd man, but now 1st lady is in the middle to begin the reel with 2nd man.

33-40 1st man leads his partner down the middle and up again.

41-48 1st and 2nd couples change places with poussette.

1st couple repeat the dance with the next couple.

THE MOUDIEWART

TUNE *Own tune or any good jig*   TIME 6/8

This is a longways jig-time dance for 3 couples. A new top couple begins on every 3rd repetition.

BARS

1-4 1st man and 2nd lady advance towards each other with 2 pas de basque, then turn each other giving right hands and return to place with 2 skip change of step.

5-8 1st lady and 2nd man do the same.

9-16 1st man leads his partner down the middle for 3 skip change of step, up for 3, then they cast off one place on their own sides of the dance.

17-20 They dance down through the 3rd couple, cast up round them, and cross over to face 1st corners.

21-24 1st couple set to 1st corners, then set to 2nd corners—4 pas de basque.

25-30 They dance reel of three with their corners, beginning the reel by giving right shoulder to 2nd corner—6 skip change of step.

31-32 1st couple cross over to own sides of the dance one place down—2 skip change of step.

1st couple repeat the dance with the next 2 couples.

92

MY ONLY JO AND DEARIE O

TUNE *Own tune or any good strathspey*   TIME 4/4

This is a longways strathspey dance for 3 couples. A new top couple begins on every 3rd repetition.

BARS

1-8   With 1st lady leading 1st, 2nd and 3rd ladies dance round behind the 3 men and return to places—8 travelling strathspey steps.

9-16   The 3 men do the same round the ladies.

17-24   1st and 2nd couples promenade round to places—8 travelling steps.

25-32   1st and 3rd couples poussette right round (*See* INTRODUCTION), 1st couple finishing in 2nd place, 2nd couple having moved up—8 strathspey setting steps.

1st couple repeat the dance with next 2 couples.

THE NEW HIGHLAND LADDIE

TUNE *Own tune or any good reel*　　　　　TIME 4/4

This is a longways reel-time dance for 3 couples. A new top couple begins on every 3rd repetition.

BARS

1-8　　1st couple, with nearer hands joined, set twice to 2nd lady, then set twice to 2nd man. They finish, with right hands joined, facing the bottom of the set.

9-16　　1st couple lead down, cross over below 2nd couple, cast behind 3rd couple and lead up the middle. They cast off one place on their wrong side and finish facing 1st corners.

17-24　　1st couple set twice to 1st corners, then set twice to 2nd corners. They finish in the middle of the dance on their own sides, facing the bottom.

25-28　　1st couple lead down to 3rd couple's place followed by 2nd and 3rd couples. They cast off and lead up to the top then quickly cast off round 2nd couple who dance up to the top.

29-32　　All 3 couples turn partner with right hand.

1st couple repeat the dance with the next 2 couples.

THE NEW TOWN OF EDINBURGH

TUNE *Any good strathspey*   TIME 4/4

This is a longways strathspey dance for 3 couples. A new top couple begins on every 3rd repetition.

BARS

1-8   1st and 2nd couples set to partner then giving right hand in passing, cross over to change places. Repeat back to places.

9-12   1st and 2nd couples set to partner, then giving right hands across to make a wheel, dance half way round.

13-16 Repeat back to places but give left hands across in the wheel.

17-24 1st man leads his partner down the middle for 2 steps, they face and set to each other. 1st man leads his partner up for 2 and they cast off one place on their own sides of the dance.

25-28 1st and 3rd couples make a circle and dance right round to the left for 4 travelling steps.

29-32 1st and 2nd couples dance right and left across and back again—one step to each hand.

1st couple repeat the dance with next 2 couples.

NONE SO PRETTY

TUNE *Own tune or any good reel*   TIME 4/4

This is a longways reel-time dance for 3 couples. A new top couple begins on every 3rd repetition.

BARS

1-4   1st couple turn each other with the right hand and cast off one place on their own sides.

5-8   They turn each other with left hand and finish 1st lady between 2nd couple who have faced down, and 1st man between 3rd couple who have faced up

9-16   All set twice, 1st couple turning right about on the last 2 steps to finish 1st lady between 2nd and 3rd men, and 1st man between 2nd and 3rd ladies. All set twice.

17-24   1st couple dance the reel of three on the sides of the dance with the 2nd and 3rd couples, 1st couple begin the reel by turning to the right and giving right shoulder. 1st couple finish back to back in the middle between the 2nd couple.

25-32   1st and 2nd couples dance reel of four across the dance and finish ready for allemande.

33-40   1st and 2nd couples allemande.

1st couple repeat the dance with next 2 couples.

ODD THOUGHTS

TUNE *Any good strathspey*   TIME 4/4

This is a longways strathspey dance for 3 couples. A new top couple begins on every 3rd repetition.

BARS

1-8   1st, 2nd and 3rd couples, giving partner right hands, cross over to change places. Repeat back to places—8 strathspey travelling steps.

9-16   1st man leads his partner down the middle and up.

17-24   1st and 2nd couples change places with allemande.

25-32   2nd, 1st and 3rd couples make a circle and dance 4 strathspey travelling steps to the left, and 4 to the right back to places.

1st couple now repeat the dance with the next 2 couples.

PERTHSHIRE HIGHLANDERS

TUNE *Own tune or any good strathspey*   TIME 4/4

This is a longways strathspey dance for 3 couples. A new top couple begins on every 3rd repetition of the dance.

BARS

1-8   1st man leads his partner—with both hands crossed in front—behind 2nd man, across below 2nd lady, round behind 3rd lady and up the middle to original places.

9-12   1st couple dance down the middle.

13-16   As they dance up again they turn each other with right hand, then with left and finish facing 1st corners. 2nd couple step up to the top.

17-24   1st couple turn 1st corners with right hand, they dance round each other passing right shoulders, turn 2nd corners with left hand and giving right hand to partner in passing, cross over to 2nd place on their own sides.

25-28   1st and 3rd couples dance 4 hands round to the left—right round.

29-32   1st and 2nd couples dance right and left, taking one step to each hand.

1st couple repeat the dance with the next 2 couples.

THE PRIEST AND HIS BOOKS

TUNE *Own tune or any good reel*   TIME 4/4

This is a longways reel-time dance for 3 couples. A new top couple begins on every 3rd repetition.

BARS

1-4   1st man, joining right hands with 3rd lady, leads her up to the top and she casts off one place on her own side of the dance. 1st man returns to place.

5-8   1st lady does the same with 3rd man.

9-12   1st and 3rd men lead their partners down the middle, 3rd couple in front.

13-16   They turn and 1st man leads his partner back to the top while 3rd couple turn each other with right hand and return to 3rd place.

17-24   1st couple cast off one place on their own side of the dance, lead down between the 3rd couple divide and cast up into 2nd place. 2nd couple move up.

1st couple repeat the dance with next 2 couples.

THE PRINCE OF ORANGE

TUNE *Come Under My Plaidie*   TIME 6/8

*This is a circle dance for 2 couples. Couples stand in a
circle round the room—those facing clockwise move in
that direction, and those facing counter-clockwise move
in a counter-clockwise direction. Odd numbers face
clockwise, even numbers counter-clockwise.*

BARS

1-8   All advance and retire twice—2 skip change
       of step forward and 2 backward twice.

9-10   Bending slightly to the left, they clap their
       hands 3 times.

11-12 Beat with the right heel 3 times (as the piper
       does).

13-16 All advance, passing right shoulder to right
       shoulder, to meet the next couple—4 skip
       change of step.

Repeat as many times as you will.

QUIET AND SNUG

TUNE *Own tune or any good strathspey*   TIME 4/4

This is a longways strathspey dance for 2 couples. A new top couple begins on every 2nd repetition.

BARS

1-4   1st couple, joining nearer hands, set twice to 2nd lady.

5-8   They turn each other, with both hands joined, twice round and finish, with nearer hands joined, facing 2nd man.

9-16   They repeat bars 1-8 with 2nd man.

17-24   1st man leads his partner down the middle for 3 steps, up for 3, then they cast off into 2nd place on their own sides, with 2 steps.

25-32   1st and 2nd couples dance right and left across and back again.

1st couple repeat the dance with the next couple.

THE RAKISH HIGHLANDMAN

TUNE *Own tune or any good jig*   TIME 6/8

This is a longways jig-time dance for 3 couples. A new top couple begins on every 3rd repetition.

BARS

1-8   1st, 2nd and 3rd couples dance the reel of three on their own side of the dance, 1st couple beginning the reel by giving right shoulders to 2nd couple.

9-16 1st man leads his partner down the middle and up again. They finish ready for allemande.

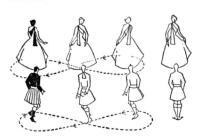

17-24   1st and 2nd couples change places with allemande, 1st couple finishing facing 1st corners.

25-32   1st couple turn 1st corner with the right hand, partner with the left, 2nd corner with the right, then turning partner with left finish back to back in the middle facing their own sides of the dance.

35-40   Double Triangles.

1st couple repeat the dance with next 2 couples.

THE ROYAL VISIT

TUNE *Any good jig*   **TIME 6/8**

This is a longways jig-time dance for 2 couples. A new top couple begins on every 2nd repetition.

BARS

1-8   1st couple set twice—4 pas de basque—and giving right hand, turn 1½ times to finish in partner's place.

9-16   1st man sets twice to 2nd lady and turns her with the right hand 1½ times to change places, while 1st lady does the same with 2nd man.

17-20   Ladies half chain. Ladies cross giving right hand then turn partners (who have stood still) half round with left hand.

21-24   Giving right hand, partners turn into positions for poussette.

25-32   1st and 2nd couples change places with poussette.

1st couple repeat the dance with next couple.

RED HOUSE

TUNE *Own tune or any suitable reel*   TIME 4/4

This is a longways reel-time dance for 2 couples. A new top couple begins on every 2nd repetition.

BARS

1-8   1st couple set and cast off one place on their own sides of the dance. They set and cast up to top again.

9-16   1st man casts off round 2nd man, crosses over above 2nd lady, dances round her and crosses to stand below 2nd man. 1st lady follows him and finishes below 2nd lady.

17-24 Now 1st lady casts up round 2nd lady, crosses to go below 2nd man, dances up round him and crosses to her own place. 1st man follows her to finish in his own place.

25-32 1st couple dance the reel of three with the 2nd man. 1st lady gives left shoulder to 2nd man to begin the reel. When she finishes the reel in 1st man's place, 1st lady crosses to her own place, while the 2 men dance one place on. 1st man is now in 2nd place.

33-40   1st couple dance the reel of three with 2nd lady. 1st lady gives 2nd lady right shoulder to begin the reel, while 1st man dances across into 2nd lady's place to enter the reel giving left shoulder to his partner. 1st man finishes the reel and dances over into 2nd place, while the 2 ladies dance one place on. 1st lady is now in 2nd place.

1st couple repeat the dance with the next couple.

SANDY O'ER THE LEA

TUNE *Any good strathspey*   **TIME** 4/4

This is a longways strathspey dance for 2 couples. A new top couple begins on every 2nd repetition.

BARS

1-8   1st and 2nd couples, giving right hands across to make a wheel, dance 4 travelling steps round, then giving left hands across, dance 4 steps back to places.

9-16   1st and 2nd couples set to partners and giving right hand in passing, cross over to change places. They repeat back to places.

17-24   1st man leads his partner down the middle followed by the 2nd couple. 1st couple turn towards each other and dance between 2nd couple who dance down then turn to follow them.

1st and 2nd couple dance up and finish ready for allemande.

25-32   1st and 2nd couples change places with allemande.

1st couple repeat the dance with the next couple.

SCOTS BONNET

TUNE *Own tune or any good jig*   TIME 6/8

This is a longways jig-time dance for 2 couples. A new top couple begins on every 2nd repetition.

BARS

1-8   1st and 2nd couples dance right and left across and back again.

9-16   1st man leads his partner down the middle and up again.

17-24   1st couple cast off one place on their own side of the dance, cross over, giving right hand in passing, and cast off round 3rd couple, then lead up to the top—8 skip change of step.

25-26   1st couple still hold right hands while 1st lady gives left hand to 2nd man and 1st man gives left hand to 2nd lady. They all set.

27-30   1st couple, dropping partner's hands turn 2nd couple into the centre to make the line again. All set.

31-32   1st couple cross over into 2nd place on their own side of the dance, 1st lady passing in front of her partner. 2nd couple dance up to the top.

1st couple repeat the dance with next couple.

THE SEAGULL

TUNE *Any good jig*   TIME 6/8

This is a longways dance for 3 couples. A new top couple begins on every 3rd repetition.

BARS

1-4   1st couple, joining right hands, turn each other, then cast off one place on their own sides of the dance—4 skip change of step.

5-8   They turn each other joining left hands and cast off another place on their own sides.

9-12   1st and 3rd couples dance half poussette to change places.

1st couple finish facing 1st corners.

13-16   1st couple set to 1st corners, then to 2nd—4 pas de basque. They use the last pas de basque to finish side by side on their own sides facing down.

17-24   1st and 3rd couples make a circle and dance 8 slip steps to the left and 8 back to the right.

25-32   With 2nd couple leading, 1st and 2nd couples promenade right round—8 skip change of step.

1st couple repeat the dance with the next 2 couples.

SHE'S OWER YOUNG TO MARRY YET

TUNE *Original or any good strathspey*   TIME 4/4

This is a longways strathspey dance for 3 couples. A new top couple begins on every 3rd repetition of the dance.

BARS

1-8   1st couple, joining nearer hands, set twice to 2nd lady who sets to them. All 3 make a circle and dance round for 4 steps finishing in a line of 3 facing 2nd man.

9-16   They set twice to 2nd man, who sets to them, then making a circle of 4 they dance round to original places.

17-24 1st couple, followed by 2nd and 3rd couples, lead down the middle to 3rd place where each couple in turn crosses over and casts up into own places on the wrong side.

25-26 All 3 couples set to partners.

27-28 1st couple cast off one place, while 2nd couple dance up one place to the top and 3rd couple set to each other.

29-32 All 3 couples turn partner with right hand 1½ times to finish on their own side of the dance.

1st couple repeat the dance with next 2 couples.

SHOULDER TO SHOULDER

TUNE *Any good jig*   **TIME 6/8**

This is a longways dance for 2 couples. A new top couple begins on every 2nd repetition of the dance.

BARS

1-8   1st couple turn each other with the right hand and return to place. They repeat turning with the left hand.

9-16   1st man leads his partner down the middle and up again but places her in the middle facing down, while he faces her. 2nd couple move forward as 1st couple pass them and stand facing each other below 1st couple to make a line ready for a reel of four.

17-24   All set twice, then turn partner once round giving 2 hands—4 pas de basque.

25-32   Reel of four up and down the dance. They finish ready for poussette.

33-40   1st and 2nd couples change places with poussette.

1st couple repeat the dance with the next couple.

TARRY A WHILE

TUNE *Own tune or any good jig* TIME 6/8

This is a longways jig-time dance for 2 couples. A new top couple begins on every 2nd repetition.

BARS

1-8 1st man turns 2nd lady with right hand and they return to places. They repeat giving left hands.

9-12 1st lady turns 2nd man with the right hand and they return to places.

13-16 1st lady and 2nd man turn with left hand but they hold on and give right hands to their own partners to make a diagonal line of 4.

17-20 All 4 set twice.

21-24 1st lady and 2nd man turn each other with left hand into the middle to face their own partner with whom they join both hands.

25-32 1st and 2nd couples change places with poussette.

1st couple repeat the dance with next couple.

TARTAN PLAIDIE

TUNE *Own tune or any good strathspey*   TIME 4/4

This is a longways strathspey dance for 2 couples. A new top couple begins on every 2nd repetition.

BARS

1-8   1st and 2nd couples, giving right hands in passing, cross over to change places—4 strathspey steps. They repeat back to places.

9-16   1st and 2nd couples, giving right hands across to make a wheel, dance round for 4 travelling steps, then giving left hand across, dance back to places for 4 steps.

17-24   1st man leads his partner down the middle and up again—finishing ready for allemande.

25-32   1st and 2nd couples change places with allemande.

1st couple repeat the dance with next couple.

THE THISTLE

TUNE *Any good 2/4 tune*

This is a longways dance for 3 couples. A new top couple begins on every 3rd repetition.

BARS

1-8   1st man leads his partner down the middle and up again.

9-16   1st couple dance the 1st figure of Petronella, but on bars 13-14 they turn into 2nd place—2nd couple having moved up—and there set to each other.

17-24   The 3 ladies join hands and the 3 men do so also. All advance and retire twice.

25-32   1st, 2nd and 3rd couples make a ring and dance 8 slip steps round to the left and 8 back again.

1st couple repeat the dance with the next 2 couples.

TODLEN HAME

TUNE *Own tune or any good jig*   TIME 6/8

This is a longways jig-time dance for 3 couples. A new top couple begins on every 3rd repetition.

BARS

1-8   1st and 2nd couples dance a reel of four. 1st lady and 2nd man begin the reel by passing with the left shoulder in the middle.

1st couple finish in 2nd couple's place.

9-16   1st, 2nd and 3rd couples dance Grand Chain, 2nd couple facing each other at the top, 1st couple facing down and 3rd couple facing up to begin the Chain.

17-24   1st and 2nd couples dance right and left across and back again.

25-32   1st couple lead down between 3rd couple, divide and cast up round them, lead up between 2nd couple and cast off on their own sides of the dance into 2nd place.

1st couple repeat the dance with next 2 couples.

A TRIP TO ABERDEEN

TUNE *Own tune or any good jig*   **TIME 6/8**

This is a longways jig-time dance for 3 couples. A new top couple begins on every 3rd repetition.

BARS

1-4   1st man casts off behind 2nd man and crosses to 3rd lady—2 skip change of steps—he joins both hands with her and turns her with 2 pas de basque to finish standing between 2nd and 3rd ladies.

5-8   1st lady does the same with 3rd man, to finish standing between the 2 men.

9-16   1st, 2nd and 3rd couples make a circle and dance 8 slip steps to the left and 8 back, 1st couple finishing facing 1st corners.

17-24   1st couple set to and turn corners, and finish between their corners.

25-28   1st lady, between 2nd and 3rd men, and 1st man between 2nd and 3rd ladies, advance and retire.

29-32   1st couple, giving 2 hands, turn each other 1½ times to finish in 2nd place on their own sides of the dance—4 pas de basque.

1st couple repeat the dance with next 2 couples.

A TRIP TO HOLLAND

TUNE *Own tune or any good strathspey*   TIME 4/4

This is a longways strathspey dance for 3 couples. A new top couple begins on every 3rd repetition.

BARS

1-8   1st and 2nd couples set twice, then giving right hand to partner cross over to change places.

9-12   1st and 2nd ladies, turning round towards each other, cast back to their own sides of the dance. They finish standing beside their partners who are now in the middle.

13-16   1st and 2nd men do the same back to their places.

17-24   1st man leads his partner down the middle, they cast up round 3rd couple then lead up the middle to the top.

25-28   1st couple cross over at the top and cast off one place on the wrong sides of the dance.

29-32   1st couple turn each other with both hands 1½ times to finish on their own sides of the dance.

1st couple repeat the dance with next couple.

TWO AND TWO

TUNE *Own tune or any good jig*   TIME 6/8

This is a longways jig-time dance for 2 couples. A new top couple begins on every 2nd repetition.

BARS

1-8   1st 2 men join nearer hands and 1st 2 ladies do the same. They set twice to partner, then giving right hand turn partner and return to place.

9-12   1st lady sets twice to 2nd lady, while 1st man sets twice to 2nd man.

13-16   1st and 2nd couples turn partner with left hand and return to place.

17-20   1st and 2nd couples make a circle and dance 8 slip steps to the left right round.

21-24   1st and 2nd couples dance back to back with partner.

25-32   1st man leads his partner down the middle for 3 steps, up for 3 and they both cast off for 2 steps on their own side of the dance.

1st couple repeat the dance with next couple.

THE VILLAGE REEL

TUNE *Own tune or any good strathspey*   TIME 4/4

This is a longways strathspey dance for 2 couples. A new top couple begins on every 2nd repetition.

BARS

1-8   1st and 2nd couples poussette right round to original places (*See* INTRODUCTION).

9-16   1st couple, with hands crossed in front, promenade round the 2nd couple finishing at the top of the dance.

17-24   1st man leads his partner down the middle and up again.

25-32   1st and 2nd couples change places with allemande.

1st couple repeat the dance with next couple.

WATSON'S REEL

TUNE *John Grumlie or any good jig*   TIME 6/8

This is a longways jig-time dance for 2 couples. A new top couple begins on every 2nd repetition.

BARS

1-8   1st and 2nd couples make a circle and dance 8 slip steps round to the left and 8 back to place.

9-16   1st man leads his partner down the middle for 3 skip change of step, up for 3, then they cast off into 2nd place for 2 steps. 2nd couple move up.

17-24   1st and 2nd couples dance right and left across and back again—2 skip change of step to each hand.

1st couple repeat the dance with the next couple.

TUNE *Any good jig*   TIME 6/8

This is a longways jig-time dance for 3 couples. A new top couple begins on every 3rd repetition.

BARS

1-4   1st man and 2nd lady advance towards each other with 2 pas de basque, then turn each other giving right hands and return to places with 2 skip change of step.

5-8   1st lady and 2nd man do the same.

9-16   1st couple dance reel of three on the opposite sides of the dance. They begin the reel by crossing over and going through the middle, 1st man giving right shoulder to 3rd lady and 1st lady left shoulder to 3rd man—8 skip change of step.

17-24 1st couple dance reel of three on their own sides, again crossing over and going through the middle to begin.

25-32 1st couple set to each other and cross over, giving right hand in passing. They cast off one place on the opposite side of the dance, then turn with left hand to finish in 2nd place on their own side.

33-40   1st and 3rd couples make a circle and dance 8 slip steps to the left and 8 back to the right.

41-48   1st and 2nd couples dance right and left across and back again.

1st couple repeat the dance with next 2 couples.

WHAT YOU PLEASE

TUNE *Any good jig*   TIME 6/8

This is a longways jig-time dance for 3 couples. A new top couple begins on every 3rd repetition of the dance.

BARS

1-4   1st and 2nd couples set, and, giving right hand in passing to partner, cross over to change places.

5-8   1st and 2nd couples, giving right hands across in a wheel, dance right round—4 skip change of step back to place.

9-16 Repeat bars 1-8 but give left hand across in the wheel.

17-24 1st man leads his partner down the middle for 3 skip change of step and up for 3. They then cast off with 2 skip change of step into 2nd place, 2nd couple moving up.

25-32 1st and 3rd couples make a circle and dance 8 slip steps round to left and 8 back again.

33-40 1st and 2nd couples dance right and left across and back again.

1st couple repeat the dance with next 2 couples.

122

WITHIN A MILE OF EDINBURGH TOON

TUNE *Own tune or any good strathspey*   TIME 4/4

This is a longways strathspey dance for 3 couples. A new couple begins on every 3rd repetition.

BARS

1-8 1st couple cast off one place on their own sides of the dance and meeting, turn each other with both hands. They cast off another place and turn again with both hands.

9-12 1st couple lead up to the top, cross over and cast off into 2nd place on the wrong side of the dance.

13-16 1st and 2nd couples dance right and left across and back again—1 step to each hand. They finish facing 1st corners.

17-24 1st couple set to and turn 1st corners, then set to and turn 2nd corners finishing between their corners.

25-28 All 3 couples advance and retire.

29-32 1st, 2nd and 3rd couples turn with both hands—1st couple turning 1½ times. All return to own side of the dance.

1st couple repeat the dance with next 2 couples.

WOO'D AND MARRIED AND A'

TUNE *Own tune or any good jig*   TIME 6/8

This is a longways jig-time dance for 3 couples. A new top couple begins on every 3rd repetition.

BARS

1-8   1st, 2nd and 3rd couples make a circle and dance 8 slip steps to the left and 8 back to places.

9-16   1st, 2nd and 3rd couples with hands crossed in front promenade right round. 1st and 2nd couples finish ready for poussette.

17-24   1st and 2nd couples change places with poussette—on the last 2 steps 1st man places his partner between the 2nd couple who have turned to face down, while he goes between 3rd couple who have faced up.

25-28   All set twice and 1st couple turn left about on the 3rd and 4th step to finish 1st lady between 2nd and 3rd ladies. 1st man between 2nd and 3rd men.

29-32   Join hands in threes again and set twice.

1st couple repeat the dance with next 2 couples.

PROGRAMME LIST

Dances unpublished by the R.S.C.D.S.

†*Dances specially suitable for children.*

REELS

Admiral Nelson, 12
†* Bonnie Geordie's Wig, 16
†* Bonny Kitty, 17
* Brechin Fancy, 18
Cadgers in the Canongate, 20
Captain McBride's Hornpipe, 23
* Captain Mackintosh, 24
* Carl Cam' Ower The Croft, 28
College Hornpipe, 29
* Countess of Lauderdale's Reel, 30
* Countess of Sutherland's Reel, 32
Fidget, 37
General Stuart's Reel, 40
Grant's Rant, 42
* Happy Returns, 43
† Johnny Groat's House, 52
†* Kelso Races, 53
* Ladies of Dingwall, 56
* Lads of Saltcoats, 58
Lady Baird's Reel, 61
Lady Mary Menzies' Reel, 66
Loch Leven Castle, 74
* Lord Eglinton's Reel, 76
Maxwell's Rant, 80
Miss Burns' Reel, 82
Miss Cholmondeley's Reel, 84

* Miss Chirsty Stewart, 85
Miss Clemy Stewart's Reel, 86
Miss Jessie Dalrymple's Reel, 88
* Monifieth Star, 91
* New Highland Laddie, 94
None So Pretty, 96
Red House, 104
* Thistle, The, 113

JIGS

† Berwick Johnnie, 13
* Edinburgh Jigs, 36
Express, The, 34
* Frog In The Middle, 38
† Highland Fair, 46
* Hooper's Jig, 44
† Isle, The, 48
Just As I Was in The Morning *or* The Deuks Dang Ower My Daddie, 50
* Kiss Under the Stairs, 55
† Lady Catherine Bruce's Reel, 62
Lassies of Dunse, 70
Leith Country Dance, 72
† Merry Reapers, 81
* Miss Margaret Hill, 89
† Miss Welsh's Reel, 90

125

Moudiewart, The, 92

Priest And His Books, 99
† Prince of Orange, 100

Rakish Highlandman, 102
* Royal Visit, 103

Scots Bonnet, 107
* Seagull, The, 108
* Shoulder to Shoulder, 110

Tarry A While, 111
Todlen Hame, 114
Trip to Aberdeen, 115
† Two and Two, 117

† Watson's Reel, 119
* What You Please, 122
* Willie's Rare And Willie's
  Fair, 120
Woo'd and Married And A',
  124

STRATHSPEYS

* The Blithest Lass That
  Ever Was Seen, 14
Bridge of Nairn, 19

Ca' The Ewes, 22

Duchess of Atholl's Slipper,
  33

I'll Gang Nae Mair To Yon
  Toon, 47

Jimmy's Fancy, 49

Keppoch's Rant, 54

Lady Auckland's Reel, 60
* Lady Charlotte Bruce, 63
Lady Jean Murray's Rant, 64
* Lady Lucy Ramsay, 65

* Lady Susan Stewart's
  Strathspey, 68
* Lass O' Loudon, 69
Learig, The, 71
Lennoxlove To Blantyre, 73
Lochiel's Rant, 75

* McLachlan's Reel, 77
Maggie Lauder, 78
* Marquis of Lorne, 79
* Miss Betty Boyle's Reel,
  83
* Miss Corbett's Strathspey,
  87
My Only Jo And Dearie O,
  93

* New Town Of Edinburgh,
  95

* Odd Thoughts, 97

Perthshire Highlanders, 98

Quiet and Snug, 101

* Sandy O'er The Lea, 106
She's Ower Young To Marry
  Yet, 109

Tartan Plaidie, 112
Trip To Holland, 116

Village Reel, 118

Within A Mile Of Edinburgh
  Toon, 123

MEDLEY
Cauld Kail, 26

SLOW 6/8 TIME
Gentle Shepherd, 39

INDEX

Admiral Nelson, 12

Berwick Johnnie, 13
Blithest Lass That Ever Was Seen, 14
Bonnie Geordie's Wig, 16
Bonnie Kitty, 17
Brechin Fancy, 18
Bridge of Nairn, 19

Ca' The Ewes, 22
Cadgers In The Canongate, 20
Captain McBride's Hornpipe, 23
Captain Mackintosh, 24
Carl Cam' Ower The Croft, 28
Cauld Kail (Medley), 26
College Hornpipe, 29
Countess of Lauderdale's Reel, 30
Countess of Sutherland's Reel, 32

Duchess Of Atholl's Slipper, 33

Edinburgh Jigs, 36
Express, The, 34

Fidget, 37
Frog In The Middle, 38

General Stuart's Reel, 40
Gentle Shepherd, 39
Grant's Rant, 42

Happy Returns, 43
Highland Fair, 46
Hooper's Jig, 44

I'll Gang Nae Mair To Yon Toon, 47
Isle, The, 48

Jimmy's Fancy, 49
Johnny Groat's House, 52
Just As I Was In The Morning *or* The Deuks Dang Ower My Daddie, 50

Kelso Races, 53
Keppoch's Rant, 54
Kiss Under The Stairs, 55

Ladies of Dingwall, 56
Lads of Saltcoats, 58
Lady Auckland's Reel, 60
Lady Baird's Reel, 61
Lady Catherine Bruce's Reel, 62
Lady Charlotte Bruce, 63
Lady Jean Murray's Rant, 64
Lady Lucy Ramsay, 65
Lady Mary Menzies' Reel, 66
Lady Susan Stewart's Strathspey, 68
Lass O' Loudon, 69
Lassies of Dunse, 70
Learig, The, 71
Leith Country Dance, 72
Lennoxlove To Blantyre, 73

127

Loch Leven Castle, 74
Lochiel's Rant, 75
Lord Eglinton's Reel, 76

McLachlan's Reel, 77
Maggie Lauder, 78
Marquis Of Lorne, 79
Maxwell's Rant, 80
Merry Reapers, 81
Miss Burns' Reel, 82
Miss Betty Boyle's Reel, 83
Miss Cholmondeley's Reel, 84
Miss Chirsty Stewart, 85
Miss Clemy Stewart's Reel, 86
Miss Corbett's Strathspey, 87
Miss Jessie Dalrymple's Reel, 88
Miss Margaret Hill, 89
Miss Welsh's Reel, 90
Monifieth Star, 91
Moudiewart, The, 92
My Only Jo And Dearie O, 93

New Highland Laddie, 94
New Town of Edinburgh, 95
None So Pretty, 96

Odd Thoughts, 97

Perthshire Highlanders, 98
Priest And His Books, 99

Prince of Orange, 100

Quiet And Snug, 101

Rakish Highlandman, 102
Red House, 104
Royal Visit, 103

Sandy O'er The Lea, 106
Scots Bonnet, 107
Seagull, The, 108
She's Ower Young To Marry Yet, 109
Shoulder to Shoulder, 110

Tarry a While, 111
Tartan Plaidie, 112
Thistle, The, 113
Todlen Hame, 114
Trip To Aberdeen, 115
Trip To Holland, 116
Two and Two, 117

Village Reel, 118

Watson's Reel, 119
What You Please, 122
Willie's Rare And Willie's Fair, 120
Within A Mile Of Edinburgh Toon, 123
Woo'd And Married And A', 124